WOMAN

Bethany Ufema

Published by Bethany and Aaron Ufema
ISBN: 978-1-7347219-0-4

womanbook.co

Cover and interior design: Aaron Ufema

A cup of water
in Jesus' name.

Isaiah 61:1

1

Did you forget
that God's reflection
looks like you?

–*Image*

2

Feel the edges
of your limitations
and ask yourself,
who made them?

3

Courage is when
faith asks fear to dance
and takes the lead.

4

Your body's been
fighting wars for you—
making love for you—
growing life in you—
honor her.

5

Your power
is in your pain,
not your pretty.

6

They've told you to stay quiet for so long,
you've forgotten to tell yourself
they were wrong.

7

Increase was the first command–
stop reducing yourself.

Genesis 1:28

8

The demons forged from disapproval
and the gods formed out of praise
are only seeking slaves.

9

Acceptance is God's river,
but you must choose to drink.

10

You were born
to give birth
to dreams.

15

Be a gold digger
who mines out the value
in herself.

16

Those who make light of you
underestimate God.

17

May the fire that gets hotter
as you refuse to bow
refine your resolve
to stand like gold.

18

Don't look for love where it isn't
because you didn't get it
where it should have been.

19

Contained within your pain
is all the progress
the world is aching
for you to bring.

20

Curiosity
is a soft, growing body
while pride remains
a shell.

–*Armor*

21

Before you break your neck
illuminating for the blind
what they have no desire to see—
ask if they want to be well.

22

If you find yourself defined
by limiting words,
grow your vocabulary.

23

What enemy
told you your body
isn't God's glory?

–Eden

24

Fear will only
lead you away
from that which must
be done.

25

Your purpose
doesn't need
permission.

26

Lowering your head
like an ostrich
is one way to survive
if you only want
a view of the dirt.

27

Move through fear
and you will realize
it is only a ghost.

28

Hell will devalue your identity
to disable your design.

29

Even if you are mocked–
so was God.

Mark 10:34

30

Your scars are raised
as an Ebenezer
for healing too costly
to be forgotten.

31

You are capable of more
than what you've overcome.

32

Repression
is the secret agent
of steady decay.

33

Use your grit
to feel your pain
rather than resist it.

34

Bonding with another
is a different thing
than being bound to another.

– Codependent

35

Your life—
even full grown—
is not another's
or your own.

−*Unity*

36

You are only "too much"
to handle
for those who believe
you need handling.

37

Train your daughter
to be adept at facing danger—
as adept at facing those who tell her
she isn't dangerous.

38

The avoidance of pain
is paralysis.

–*Stuck*

39

Coming to grips with your motives
is learning to face your wounds.

40

You are not waiting to be healed
by the hands that hurt you–
you are waiting to realize
they are not that powerful.

41

Forgiveness
is not a destination
but a process
of becoming.

42

You are the advantage
in love and war.

43

God did not send
a reinforcement
that is weaker.

–*Ezer kenegdo*

Genesis 2:8

44

Challenge
every constraint
that contradicts
your competencies.

45

Stay awake –
wide awake –
what God woke,
no thief can take.

46

The easy road is never
downhill from here.

47

Settling down with a lie
is as hazardous
as sleepwalking.

48

You cannot go around
what you must go through–
and no bottle or cake or man
can carry you.

49

God is a surgeon—
not an anesthesiologist.

50

When you feel weak
because you cried,
remember it's resilience
that floods your eyes.

51

It does not matter
how narrowly you escaped
now that you have.

52

If this journey
requires more strength
than you wanted to need,
you are becoming stronger
than you ever dreamed.

53

Even God wears battle scars.

John 20:27

54

Offering God your grief—
like lifting gravity—
is the weightiest act
of intimacy.

55

You are a well so deep
you couldn't possibly be defined
so shallowly.

56

Don't settle for water
from someone else's cup
now that you know
it's time to dig a well.

57

Wherever you lost yourself,
go back for her
so you can stop looking to be found
in someone else.

58

Your genesis
was the beginning
of partnership.

Genesis 2:24

59

God did not light
the lamp of your spirit
to say to the flame,
this is your limit.

60

Perfection is a poison
meant to paralyze your progress.

61

Anxiety
is the flight of surrender
clutched tightly.

–Control

62

Never feel guilty
that coming closer to yourself
may leave behind those
who want someone else.

63

Regret
is a fruit of
self-neglect.

64

"Bossy" = authoritative
"ice queen" = objective
"emotional" = empathetic
(what they meant).

65

No stereotype
is the prototype
of your person.

66

Turn over every rock
and the other cheek–
never a blind eye.

–*Justice and mercy*

67

You've been called "helper"
for so long
it's been long forgotten
that is a name of God's.

–Ezer

68

In waiting for permission
you may be withholding it
from someone else.

69

In case you neglected to ask:
what do you think?
how do you feel?
what do you want?

70

If your heart and mind
don't resolve their differences
you will forever embody
this kind of

dissonance.

71

Let God till
your soil down deep –
the roots of your future
generations will reap.

72

Don't go through this whole life
never loving the body
that served you to the end.

73

Your beauty
is God's likeness—
not man's décor.

74

God flips tables
in the same Spirit
God empties graves.

WOMAN

75

Full participation in the bedroom
but not the boardroom
is the perverted idea of
"separate but equal."

76

The rocks your generations
hid beneath
are those you must
turn over.

–*Inheritance*

77

The harder the ground,
the softer the landing—
a foundation dug deep
and the house is still standing.

78

With each truth that fills
the air with your breath,
corruption chokes on
its own silent death.

79

You are filled with the breath of God—
exhale.

80

Stop holding the coattails
of the ones who hurt you
as if they would turn around
and heal you.

81

Fleeing may be necessary,
but never let it be
from yourself.

82

You are sharp like lightning
you roll like thunder
you surge like tidewater
that pulls love under
you are soft like rainfall
you are gravity's moon–
a butterfly wing's whisper
and the aftermath typhoon.

–*Love poem*

83

God is connecting your dots
like constellations
guiding generations.

84

Rejection cannot take
the key to letting love in
when the door is yours
to open.

85

Belonging
begins in
your body.

–*Home*

86

Despite who whistles
you are not the service dog.

87

Your beauty is inherent,
not a condition.

88

Pain must be felt
but not quickly obeyed.

89

Perfection is pretending.

90

Let the scandal of your life
be how you threw yourself
at God.

–For the woman who loved

Luke 7:45

91

Your body
is more than your sexuality–
it's your hospital bed–
it's your childhood home.

92

You are no
side piece of meat
up for consumption
to those who would eat.

93

Boys being boys
is not the same as
girls being toys.

94

Is the picture you're painting
with your life
one you wish to hang?

95

May whatever you lose
finally prove
it could never have made you
complete.

96

You can never be known
by comparison
or reduced
by opinion.

97

Now that you know love,
what is left to lose
or earn?

98

God pulled you from man's side—
not his behind.

Genesis 2:22

WOMAN

99

God is always flipping the script
on those writing it.

100

Don't look for water
in empty wells
that are just as thirsty as you.

101

Don't mistake overachieving
with overcoming.

102

If you were ever made to wonder
how you should be treated by a brother
look no further
than how God treats God.

103

Those you select
are chosen through
the lens of self-respect.

104

Don't squander
what you've been created for
by burying in a field
what you've been afraid to do.

105

Remember when God told you
to get out of the kitchen.

Luke 10:42

106

Equality
cannot be found
on uneven ground.

107

Dishonor
is only a reflection
of the distributor.

108

Where God knelt at your feet
it was written
what kept men from
exploiting women.

–For the woman used

John 8:8

109

God does not run
a gentlemen's club.

110

Acceptance
may be the hardest battle
ever won.

111

In a baptism of fire
you are born from God's water–
sure as a firstborn daughter.

–Refining

112

Your capacity to feel
reflects that of your arms
for folding others into them.

113

Teach a man
how much strength it takes
to let the heart break.

114

Hierarchy is a curse
God's Spirit does reverse.

115

Equality is so holy
God's own back served
to elevate the lowly.

John 19:17

116

It is better to stand tall, alone—
than shrink for someone.

117

In the name of integrity
have you ever considered
you're cheating yourself?

118

Desperation
won't make empty promises
more genuine.

119

No love can reach
the places you don't—
no kindness embrace
the places you won't.

120

God revealed
the purpose of privilege
by laying it down.

121

You have the advantage of being
the most underestimated weapon
in all creation.

122

As hell tries to mar your image
it cannot veil God's
staring back, unflinching.

123

Triumph
and accomplishment
only drive away
those you've outgrown.

124

It is better to be alone
with yourself
than remain a stranger
with someone else.

125

At what yield sign
did you leave yourself behind?

126

Your daughters learn their value
from what you are willing to tolerate.

127

Your sons learn your value
from what you are willing to tolerate.

128

The parts of you
that you neglect
will find a home
behind any broken door
left open.

129

Don't try to heal yourself
by funneling your love
through a man.

–*Depreciation*

130

Know your enemy
so hell doesn't divert you
with a decoy.

131

Turn the fingers that you're pointing
into open hands for serving
and closed fists for warring.

132

Hell will use
God's own name
to justify all it will
wrongfully claim.

133

You are not one of the animals
humankind was given dominion over.

Genesis 1:26

134

Darkness is
a tomb
or a womb.

–*Choose*

135

Sometimes it takes
having nothing left to bury
to be made ready.

–Follow God

136

Learn to speak
just as your sons did
from the day they were born.

137

Honorable is a man
who opens doors
of opportunity
and pulls out
executive chairs.

−Chivalry

138

God is not sexist—
or racist—
or corrupt—
like hell.

139

It is someone else's shame
that wants to tuck you away.

140

Your body
is not a commodity
made common
by commentary.

141

Your body
is a temple
where acts of worship
are consensual.

−The marriage bed

142

The narrative that only you
need rescuing
or protecting
overlooks your resumé.

143

Don't live off pieces of yourself
so that someone else
can feel competent
completing you.

144

Like a seed that hides
the blueprint of a tree
God unveils grandeur
through obscurity.

145

The difference between
a pipe dream and prophesy
is only discerned
while moving toward each.

146

Put on compassion
in the order you would
an oxygen mask.

147

All you need
is enough breath
for the next one.

148

When God satisfies your thirst
there is plenty left
for pouring out.

149

Healed people
heal people.

150

Striving for approval
is like repeatedly paying
for what you already own.

151

Don't reject abuse
only to give it to yourself.

152

God is not preferential
in God's treatment
of God's image.

153

Be patient with those
who have mistaken you
for someone lesser–
for those who believe
someone could be lesser
have also mistaken God.

154

Be aware of those
posing as an oasis
entirely intending
to suck you dry.

155

Anyone wanting parts of you–
and compliance from you–
is looking to be god
to an object
of his making.

156

God did not
give you dominion
that God did not
intend to commission.

Genesis 1:28

157

It takes a holy rage
to flip the tables
and the page.

–*Change*

158

It is easy to underestimate
that you only control your choices
and easy to underestimate
how much control that is.

159

Let difficulty
illuminate
your ability.

160

When you ask what all
the crushing was for
God fills your glass
with wine to pour.

161

Acceptance doesn't yell
hands up –
it whispers
palms up.

162

Your failures are the fuel
by which redemption rises.

163

Every battle you win
is a victory multiplied
through those watching.

164

Your internal dialogue
prophesies over you
constantly.

165

There's a thousand eyes on you—
both heaven and hell,
with bated breath—
waiting to see what you'll do.

166

God may sharpen you
down to dust
so all that survives
is your trust.

167

Pain is energy
that can be burned as fuel
for climbing its mountains.

168

God opens the mind
like the eyes of the blind–
and in a flash flood of light
go the floodgates of sight.

–*Revelation*

169

Righteous anger
is the lightning that strikes
before the clap
of redemption rolls in.

170

If you dare to play
the "what-if" game:
what if you grow?
what if you gain?
what if you win?

171

Fear is not a
personality trait.

172

Be aware of those
who would push you down
in order to prop up
their own egos.

173

Be aware of those
who would control you
in order to control
their own lust.

174

Humankind, in parallel lines
have symmetry with God's imagery–
but there is no hierarchy
within the Trinity.

175

It is not good for man to be alone—
even in the boardroom.

–*Ezer kenegdo*

Genesis 2:18

176

Above all else
know yourself.

177

Do not seek attention
without discerning intention.

178

More than a worthy opponent,
you are a worthy partner.

179

The difference between
overpowered and empowered
is measured, bridged, braved
within.

180

Speak to your mothers—
sisters—
daughters—
all the words
you needed to hear.

181

Freedom demands you address
all fear would suppress.

182

The fire inside of you
will not survive
burning the fuel of
another's lamp.

183

You are the image of God–
not the excess of man.

Genesis 1:27

184

Revenge
has never changed outcomes
like redemption.

185

You will never reach yourself
or anyone else
pointing fingers.

186

Be aware of those
who resist your growth
because your fullness
terrifies their scarcity.

187

You didn't come this far
to be told,
that's far enough.

188

God does not quench
the fires God lights.

189

Don't feel guilty
that your freedom
will cause the old world to grieve
its loss of control.

190

Being validated
pales in comparison
to being yourself.

191

Don't apologize
for femininity:
that you had empathy—
or loved tenderly—
or saw complexity—
in what was judged
too simply.

192

Outside forces
may limit your choices
but never can silence
our voices.

–For K.W.

193

Ready for battle—
sound the war cry—
free your tongue
to testify.

194

Jealousy
is a gross underestimation
of who you are.

195

Competitors
come by comparison
and sisters
by celebration.

196

The eyes through which
you see yourself
you see everyone
and everything else.

197

Shame would flee
if you were to learn
by treading through it
you do not burn.

198

You may perplex
as God's image
is complex.

199

When God said,
let Us make humankind in Our image–
God wasn't conversing with men.

Genesis 1:26

200

Emotions
cannot be exiled
from their own home.

201

It is not your job to change
anyone but yourself
continually.

– Grow

202

Use your imagination
to envision—
not pretend.

203

Your pulse
is the gentle reminder
to get moving.

204

Honesty
demands courage—
denial,
nothing.

205

Remember:
flattery only has
its own interests in mind.

206

The unexamined life
is already buried.

207

Every learned guide
has spent significant time
searching wilderness.

208

Help is on the way
even if it means
you must find it.

209

Shared weakness yields
contagious strength.

210

Should you descend the abyss—
look hell in the eye—
you will return to learn
you shall survive

and survive

and survive.

211

When you realize your power–
individually and in solidarity–
you will no longer accept the saying:
this is a man's world.

212

No one needs to validate
what God has authorized
from the beginning.

Genesis 1:26

213

God did not fill you
for you to fill
another's form.

214

What did you think
when you began–
that all would go
according to plan?

–*Resilience*

215

Pain is a servant
and anger a work horse
when put to good use.

216

Those who cause harm
ring the alarm
of their own pain.

217

Choose those
who wield their strength
to embrace and elevate—
not emaciate.

218

Boundaries
are a better friend
than diamonds.

219

You are no object
up for sale
to the highest bidder
of attention.

220

You are not small
like someone else's thinking.

221

The fire inside of you
is not meant to consume
but illuminate.

222

Breakthrough is the sound
of breaking down –
of all your walls
hitting ground.

223

The end of yourself
is the remnant
from which you will emerge.

224

Your rise
is the opposite
of a man's downfall.

225

Heaven advances
as you do.

226

God has never hung a sign that says:
no girls allowed.

227

It will only matter
that glass ceilings shatter
when you also obtain a ladder.

228

The truth that sets you free
will often hurt like hell.

229

Happiness flees
a forecast of rain
but hope can withstand
a downpour of pain.

230

Only God knows
who is at stake
if you stand down
instead of up.

231

Hell wouldn't have done its utmost
to keep you silent
if it wasn't so terrified
of what you'd say.

232

When you and the mirror
come to blows
the black eye inside
of you shows.

233

Love can only
bind the fractures
you let it near.

234

Unhealthy habits
are the simple sum
of unmet needs
acting out.

235

Weakness
never becomes strength
in those who hold it
at arm's length.

236

Hell will keep you
from reclaiming
all it can convince you
was never yours.

237

All truth needs
is a crack in the wall
to come crashing in
like a wrecking ball.

—Prisons

238

Repeat to your pain
what only you hold
the power to say.

239

By neglecting yourself
your needs go unmet
in someone else.

240

It is worth trading in
what has soothed you
for what will heal you.

241

As iron sharpens iron,
may the chains you are wearing
be forged into tools.

−For B.T.

Proverbs 27:17

242

Shame at your table
will eat repentance for lunch.

243

Hell will project its own lust
onto your skin
and accuse you of sin.

244

Where pain yields to praise
grows a medicine tree
with healing roots
that serve curative tea.

245

Show a man
how beautiful he can be.

246

"Ladylike"
is a general term
for what makes those around you
more comfortable.

247

Live in such a way
that hell is insecure
when you walk into the room.

248

"Your place" remains
wherever God is.

249

God is no respecter of persons
nor is God discriminant.

250

You were not made to fold
into someone else's ego.

251

You are not the lust
or the weakness
some feel around you.

252

Half-truths
are whole lies
that will lull you to sleep
in a costume of light.

253

Love will hold up
truth like a mirror
when a sister
has something in her teeth.

254

God cannot demean you–
reduce you–
debase you–
abuse you–
as God cannot cheapen
God's image.

255

When God dwelled with us twice
God told you first.

*—For the mother of Jesus
and the women at the tomb*

256

It is not your job to hide
when someone's ego feels threatened.

257

Compromise
when it comes to restaurants
but not in your taste
for mutual respect.

258

Maybe depression
is suppressed grief
and anxiety
suppressed action.

.

259

Hell would rather you go quietly–
compliantly–
than learn the art of war.

260

Those who strive
to preserve their own privilege
are still slaves
to themselves.

261

Disempowerment
is always dangerous—
and gravely so
when God is credited.

262

Hell would like to mock your beauty
by reducing its definition
and calling it seduction.

263

Whoever thinks your competence
should be sacrificed
on the altar of compliance
is burning an incense
unto themselves.

264

You are not the simulation—
you are the creation.

Genesis 1:27

265

God wouldn't rest
until you.

Genesis 2:2

266

When acceptance becomes
the final pillow
for your head,
you will stop lying awake
on rocks.

267

God makes gardens of tombs,
turning graves into wombs,
and out of your void–
revival blooms.

268

God was not given wholly to you
to be partially expressed through you.

Joel 2:28

269

May your daughter learn
as a child
to never domesticate
what would master the wild.

–*Dominion*

270

Forgiveness
prevents every evil
from having an afterlife
in you.

271

The gift of healing another
is the fruit of your pain
harvested by acceptance.

272

Allow a hard truth
to soften your heart
over time.

273

Your capacity for empathy
is healed injury
as God's scars
embrace the world.

Isaiah 53:5

274

Pain left on the back burner
will take the curtains first—
then the house—
then the neighbor's.

275

Go through the emotions
instead of the motions.

276

Be gentle with your body
that has no choice
but to be vulnerable with you.

277

Your beauty is not
in the eye of your beholder
but in the image of your Maker.

278

Don't snuff out hope
in light of disappointment
when that is the very light
it glimmers beneath.

279

The dead end
is not the end
as long as you're alive.

280

Worrying
is like taking on debt
for what you never intend
to own.

281

You'll keep running into
what you're running from
but won't run through.

– Circles

282

The subtleties
of your devaluation
matter significantly.

−Pay attention

283

Don't let anyone mistake
the metal of your weapon
for a trophy.

284

Hope can be harvested
from shared pain.

285

The extended arm of compassion
has a calloused hand of resilience.

286

A roof over your head
is no reason to make a home
beneath an oppressive ceiling.

287

Moving on
is only temporarily
more painful than staying.

–*Abuse*

288

Until you find
representation in God,
you'll keep looking for yourself
in men.

289

Rejection itself
can build the resilience
you always needed
to move on.

290

Paralyzed–
powerless–
silent–
all words secured on
the epitaph of hell.

291

You are a warrior
made to rise continually
in the face of opposition.

292

Don't mistake love
with what lacks respect.

293

Fragility
couldn't be further from
femininity.

294

When a bad seed is sown
in your good soil
the apple that falls
will nourish nations.

295

God's ultimate revenge
is complete redemption.

296

Remember:
repentance means
to change one's mind–
not one's tactic.

– *"Sorry"*

297

Quit making lemonade
out of your lemons
and uproot the lemon tree.

298

Whatever you need to hear
say it to yourself—
say it to yourself—
say it to yourself—
so that you'll believe it
when you hear it.

299

Honor her
as a warrior,
lover,
mother,
other.

–Your body

300

Hatred is
the smallest conclusion
of all.

301

Love has—
and is—
the last word.

—Tetelestai

John 19:30

302

As you consider criticism,
consider its source.

303

Decide in advance
who will win
the war within.

304

Braver than the pursuit
of the expanse of stars
is she who is willing
to face the expanse of herself.

305

Pain is a portal
through former limitations,
opening doors
to profound revelations.

306

Resurrection
happens when
you lose sight
of where you end
and God begins.

307

You weren't born for a reason—
you were born for a billion.

308

God folded
mysteries into you
and she who seeks
finds.

309

Let your beauty sink in
and well up from within,
flooding your skin.

310

If you find yourself
without a seat,
find the table
where God sits.

311

Let opposition remind you
why you spoke up to begin with.

312

It is you who must learn
to heed your crying
before she learns
no one is coming.

313

Keep pain pliant
in the water of your tears
so a hardening of soul
won't crystallize your fears.

—Bitterness

314

Love does not settle–
it propels.

WOMAN

315

I win
is nothing compared to
we won.

316

Remember:
willful ignorance
is not innocence.

–*Enabler*

317

Accept the rejection
that comes with
rejecting harm.

318

How do you treat yourself
behind closed doors?

319

It is never too late
to stand up
for the child within–
struck down.

320

The fruit of injury
is resilience
and its resurrection
empathy.

321

Your endurance will outlive
what has always
underestimated you.

322

Humanity
traded unity
for hierarchy
and called it order.

–*The fall*

323

God's thoughts are higher
than the ones that limit you.

324

How you steward
what you are given
will not be measured
by what you suppress.

325

At the commissioning of humanity
you were not instructed differently
and in the pouring of the Spirit
you are filled up equally.

Genesis 1:28
Acts 2:18

326

Don't neglect
the sober act of maturing
as you age.

327

Not all attention
is created equal.

328

Grace is the lean
that comes from a limp –
strength is the number
that carries you.

–*Sisters*

329

In the deepest of droughts
pour out praise —
a new life to dry bones
that no water could raise.

330

Treat yourself
the way you want to be treated.

331

Show her a future so powerful
your daughter will forget
her genetic memory.

332

Keeping you beneath
keeps hell on top.

333

Even God was oppressed
with confidence.

Luke 22:63

334

Freedom will cost you
all the attachment
of your bondage.

335

Sometimes resurrection
looks like walking away
from expensive graves.

–*Costly*

336

As the cycle of
refining repeats,
everything that
God starts
God completes.

−*Masterpiece,*
          for A.H.

337

The treasure God buried
within your ground
has never been lost
but must be found.

338

Split from dust and bone,
you are the divine remedy
for alone.

–*Ezer kenegdo*

Genesis 2:18

339

In pain your body knows
to deliver miracles.

–Learn from her

340

What you've been given
is not a fixed limitation
but a seed for multiplication.

341

Every road you've paved
began a jungle braved.

–*Trailblazer*

342

Insecurity
would wrap you in a dungeon
and call it a castle.

– "*Confidence*"

343

Blame is the
assassin of change.

344

No permission
can give you
what you don't claim
and no limitation
can take
what you do.

345

Your purpose is not passive.

346

"Womanhood" and
"manhood"
cannot be reduced
to a disposition
or position
or prescription.

347

Every great man
you stood behind
could have been greater
had you stood beside.

348

When you break free
you will miss the ceiling
until you learn
it is not the expanse—
but the limits—
that are threatening.

—*Never go back*

349

Comfort zones–
not war zones–
will take you out.

350

Become your own safe home
where there are no rugs
for sweeping under.

351

Until you
go back for her
you'll continue to cope
as the child you were.

352

Paying attention
is more beneficial
than seeking it.

353

The choice of who
you give power to
remains with you.

354

People-pleasing
is the fracturing
of your authentic
beginning.

355

Those who cannot celebrate you
are not ready for their own victory.

356

You could save yourself
with a word of kindness
spoken at the right time
into the mirror.

357

When you see your value
you redeem your mother—
and your mother's mother—
and any woman
made to be an object
or a product
or a victim—
you redeem their image
as you see God's.

358

Some heirlooms
deserve to be broken.

−Chain breaker

359

You are your mother's
surrogate healer.

– Generations

360

Those who cannot
look you in the eye
have not beheld
God's face.

361

Power
is for empowering
the powerless.

362

Defy the odds
burning whatever
lights you on fire.

−*Rocket fuel*

363

A future generation
is giving thanks
for your noncompliance.

364

It's not just a hellion
who leads a rebellion
but every daughter
charged by heaven.

365

When God is standing
at the door
who else is it
you're waiting for?

My deepest gratitude to:

my husband, Aaron: my partner, my lover, my constant, my home. For seeing me through the dark, for elevating every dream, for opening your life wide to mine. You've always fought so hard for us. You're the greatest example to our children. Thank you for your devotion to this project as though it were born of your own heart. Thank you for loving me like that.

my bff, Jen Muncy: for loving my guts whole. For pointing me back to true north. For being the safest place in joy and sadness. Thank you for laboring with me through the seasons within and without these pages.

Brian Towers: without your guidance, this book and its meaning would have eluded me. There aren't words of gratitude sufficient for helping me uncover, love, and become my truest self.

the midwives, who helped deliver this work with loving intuition: Krissy Donahoe, Olivia Hall, Jennifer McGill, Jen Muncy, Courtney Scholl, Becca Rowe, Emily Brown, Emily Smith, Angela Larsen, Alisha Henley, Jen Pickwell. You give me so much courage. Your insight and belief changed these pages, as it changes me.

Kristie Wahlquist: for reciprocal strength and boundless bravery: John 1:5.

my pastors, Daniel and Tammie Floyd: for your love. For the opportunities unmerited. For watering seeds in me I didn't see. You've shown me how to dream.

my God: my breath. I could never speak Your worth. You simply have my life. You have everything I am and all I will become. I am Your lamp, and You've lit me on fire. I will always burn for You.

CPSIA information can be obtained
at www.ICGtesting.com
Printed in the USA
LVHW021309101220
673819LV00021B/559